JOHN MILTON

Selected
Poems

BLOOMSBURY
* POETRY *
CLASSICS

CENTRAL

2 250 540 21

This selection by Ian Hamilton
first published 1996
Copyright © 1996 by Bloomsbury Publishing Plc

Bloomsbury Publishing Plc, 2 Soho Square,
London W1V 6HB

A CIP catalogue record for this book
is available from the British Library

ISBN 07475 2918 3

Typeset in Great Britain by
Hewer Text Composition Services, Edinburgh
Printed in Great Britain by St Edmundsbury Press, Suffolk
Jacket design by Jeff Fisher

CONTENTS

ON THE MORNING OF CHRIST'S NATIVITY

I

This is the month, and this the happy morn
Wherein the Son of Heaven's eternal King,
Of wedded maid and virgin mother born,
Our great redemption from above did bring;
For so the holy sages once did sing,
    That he our deadly forfeit should release,
And with his Father work us a perpetual peace.

II

That glorious form, that light unsufferable,
And that far-beaming blaze of majesty,
Wherewith he wont at Heaven's high council-table
To sit the midst of Trinal Unity,
He laid aside; and here with us to be,
    Forsook the courts of everlasting day,
And chose with us a darksome house of mortal clay.

III

Say Heavenly Muse, shall not thy sacred vein
Afford a present to the Infant God?
Hast thou no verse, no hymn, or solemn strain,
To welcome him to this his new abode,
Now while the heaven, by the sun's team untrod,
    Hath took no print of the approaching light,
And all the spangled host keep watch in squadrons
    bright?

IV

See how from far upon the eastern road
The star-led wizards haste with odours sweet.
O run, prevent them with thy humble ode,
And lay it lowly at his blessed feet;
Have thou the honour first thy Lord to greet,
   And join thy voice unto the Angel quire
From out his secret altar toucht with hallowed fire.

THE HYMN
I

It was the winter wild,
While the Heaven-born child
All meanly wrapt in the rude manger lies;
Nature in awe to him
Had doffed her gaudy trim,
With her great Master so to sympathize:
It was no season then for her
To wanton with the sun, her lusty paramour.

II

Only with speeches fair
She woos the gentle air
To hide her guilty front with innocent snow,
And on her naked shame,
Pollute with sinful blame,
The saintly veil of maiden white to throw,
Confounded that her Maker's eyes
Should look so near upon her foul deformities.

8

III

But he her fears to cease,
Sent down the meek-eyed Peace,
She crowned with olive green came softly sliding
Down through the turning sphere
His ready harbinger,
With turtle wing the amorous clouds dividing,
And waving wide her myrtle wand
She strikes a universal peace through sea and land.

IV

No war, or battle's sound
Was heard the World around,
The idle spear and shield were high up hung;
The hooked chariot stood
Unstained with hostile blood,
The trumpet spake not to the armed throng;
And kings sat still with awful eye,
As if they surely knew their sovereign lord was by.

V

But peaceful was the night
Wherein the Prince of light
His reign of peace upon the earth began.
The winds with wonder whist
Smoothly the waters kissed,
Whispering new joys to the mild Ocean,
Who now hath quite forgot to rave,
While birds of calm sit brooding on the charmed wave.

VI

The stars with deep amaze
Stand fixed in steadfast gaze,
Bending one way their precious influence,
And will not take their flight,
For all the morning light,
Or Lucifer that often warned them thence;
But in their glimmering orbs did glow,
Until their Lord himself bespake and bid them go.

VII

And though the shady gloom
Had given day her room,
The sun himself withheld his wonted speed,
And hid his head for shame,
As his inferior flame
The new enlightened world no more should need;
He saw a greater sun appear
Than his bright throne or burning axletree could bear.

VIII

The shepherds on the lawn,
Or ere the point of dawn,
Sat simply chatting in a rustic row;
Full little thought they then
That the mighty Pan
Was kindly come to live with them below;
Perhaps their loves, or else their sheep,
Was all that did their silly thoughts so busy keep.

IX

When such music sweet
Their hearts and ears did greet,
As never was by mortal finger strook,
Divinely-warbled voice
Answering the stringed noise,
As all their souls in blissful rapture took.
The air such pleasure loth to lose
With thousand echoes still prolongs each heavenly close.

X

Nature that heard such sound
Beneath the hollow round
Of Cynthia's seat the airy region thrilling,
Now was almost won
To think her part was done
And that her reign had here its last fulfilling;
She knew such harmony alone
Could hold all Heaven and Earth in happier union.

XI

At last surrounds their sight
A globe of circular light,
That with long beams the shame-faced night arrayed;
The helmed cherubim
And sworded seraphim
Are seen in glittering ranks with wings displayed,
Harping in loud and solemn quire
With unexpressive notes to Heaven's new-born heir.

XII

Such music (as 'tis said)
Before was never made,
But when of old the sons of morning sung,
While the Creator great
His constellations set,
And the well-balanced world on hinges hung,
And cast the dark foundations deep,
And bid the weltering waves their oozy channel keep.

XIII

Ring out ye crystal spheres,
Once bless our human ears
(If ye have power to touch our senses so)
And let your silver chime
Move in melodious time;
And let the bass of Heaven's deep organ blow,
And with your ninefold harmony
Make up full consort to th'angelic symphony.

XIV

For if such holy song
Enwrap our fancy long,
Time will run back, and fetch the age of gold,
And speckled vanity
Will sicken soon and die,
And leprous sin will melt from earthly mould,
And Hell itself will pass away,
And leave her dolorous mansions to the peering day.

XV

Yea truth and justice then
Will down return to men,
Orbed in a rainbow; and like glories wearing
Mercy will sit between
Throned in celestial sheen,
With radiant feet the tissued clouds down steering,
And Heaven as at some festival,
Will open wide the gates of her high palace hall.

XVI

But wisest Fate says no,
This must not yet be so,
The babe lies yet in smiling infancy,
That on the bitter cross
Must redeem our loss;
So both himself and us to glorify.
Yet first to those ychained in sleep
The wakeful trump of doom must thunder through the
    deep,

XVII

With such a horrid clang
As on Mount Sinai rang
While the red fire and smouldering clouds out brake.
The aged earth aghast
With terror of that blast
Shall from the surface to the centre shake,
When at the world's last session
The dreadful Judge in middle air shall spread his throne.

XVIII

And then at last our bliss
Full and perfect is,
But now begins; for from this happy day
Th'old dragon underground
In straiter limits bound,
Not half so far casts his usurped sway,
And wrath to see his kingdom fail
Swindges the scaly horror of his folded tail.

XIX

The oracles are dumb,
No voice or hideous hum
Runs through the arched roof in words deceiving.
Apollo from his shrine
Can no more divine,
With hollow shriek the steep of Delphos leaving.
No nightly trance, or breathed spell,
Inspires the pale-eyed priest from the prophetic cell.

XX

The lonely mountains o'er,
And the resounding shore,
A voice of weeping heard and loud lament;
From haunted spring, and dale
Edged with poplar pale,
The parting genius is with sighing sent;
With flower-inwoven tresses torn
The nymphs in twilight shade of tangled thickets mourn.

XXI

In consecrated earth,
And on the holy hearth,
The Lars and Lemures moan with midnight plaint,
In urns and altars round,
A drear and dying sound
Affrights the flamens at their service quaint;
And the chill marble seems to sweat,
While each peculiar power forgoes his wonted seat.

XXII

Peor and Baalim
Forsake their temples dim,
With that twice-battered god of Palestine,
And mooned Ashtaroth,
Heaven's queen and mother both,
Now sits not girt with tapers' holy shine;
The Libyc Hammon shrinks his horn,
In vain the Tyrian maids their wounded Thammuz mourn.

XXIII

And sullen Moloch fled,
Hath left in shadows dread
His burning idol all of blackest hue;
In vain with cymbals' ring
They call the grisly king,
In dismal dance about the furnace blue;
The brutish gods of Nile as fast,
Isis and Orus and the dog Anubis haste.

XXIV

Nor is Osiris seen
In Memphian grove or green,
Trampling the unshowered grass with lowings loud;
Nor can he be at rest
Within his sacred chest,
Nought but profoundest Hell can be his shroud;
In vain with timbrelled anthems dark
The sable-stoled sorcerers bear his worshipped ark.

XXV

He feels from Juda's land
The dreaded infant's hand,
The rays of Bethlehem blind his dusky eyn;
Nor all the gods beside
Longer dare abide,
Not Typhon huge ending in snaky twine.
Our babe to show his godhead true
Can in his swaddling bands control the damned crew.

XXVI

So when the sun in bed,
Curtained with cloudy red,
Pillows his chin upon an orient wave,
The flocking shadows pale
Troop to th'infernal jail,
Each fettered ghost slips to his several grave,
And the yellow-skirted fays
Fly after the night-steeds, leaving their moon-loved maze.

But see the Virgin blest
Hath laid her babe to rest.
Time is our tedious song should here have ending;
Heaven's youngest teemed star
Hath fixed her polished car,
Her sleeping Lord with handmaid lamp attending;
And all about the courtly stable
Bright-harnessed angels sit in order serviceable.

SONNET

O Nightingale, that on yon bloomy spray
    Warbl'st at eve, when all the woods are still,
    Thou with fresh hope the lover's heart dost fill,
    While the jolly hours lead on propitious May;
Thy liquid notes that close the eye of day,
    First heard before the shallow cuckoo's bill
    Portend success in love; O if Jove's will
    Have linked that amorous power to thy soft lay,
Now timely sing, ere the rude bird of hate
    Foretell my hopeless doom in some grove nigh:
    As thou from year to year hast sung too late
For my relief; yet hadst no reason why,
    Whether the Muse, or Love, call thee his mate,
    Both them I serve, and of their train am I.

ON SHAKESPEARE

What needs my Shakespeare for his honoured
   bones
The labour of an age in piled stones,
Or that his hallowed relics should be hid
Under a star-ypointing pyramid?
Dear son of memory, great heir of fame,
What needst thou such weak witness of thy name?
Thou in our wonder and astonishment
Hast built thyself a livelong monument.
For whilst to th'shame of slow-endeavouring art,
Thy easy numbers flow, and that each heart
Hath from the leaves of thy unvalued book
Those Delphic lines with deep impression took,
Then thou our fancy of itself bereaving,
Dost make us marble with too much conceiving;
And so sepulchered in such pomp dost lie,
That kings for such a tomb would wish to die.

Blest pair of sirens, pledges of Heaven's joy,
Sphere-born harmonious sisters, Voice and Verse,
Wed your divine sounds, and mixed power employ
Dead things with inbreathed sense able to pierce
And to our high-raised phantasy present
That undisturbed song of pure consent,
Aye sung before the sapphire-coloured throne
To him that sits thereon
With saintly shout and solemn jubilee,
Where the bright seraphim in burning row
Their loud up-lifted angel trumpets blow,
And the cherubic host in thousand quires
Touch their immortal harps of golden wires,
With those just spirits that wear victorious palms,
Hymns devout and holy psalms
Singing everlastingly;
That we on earth with undiscording voice
May rightly answer that melodious noise;
As once we did, till disproportioned sin
Jarred against nature's chime, and with harsh din
Broke the fair music that all creatures made
To their great Lord, whose love their motion swayed
In perfect diapason, whilst they stood
In first obedience, and their state of good.
O may we soon again renew that song,
And keep in tune with Heaven, till God ere long
To his celestial consort us unite,
To live with him, and sing in endless morn of light.

SONNET

Methought I saw my late espoused saint
   Brought to me like Alcestis from the grave,
   Whom Jove's great son to her glad husband gave,
   Rescued from death by force though pale and faint.
Mine as whom washed from spot of child-bed taint,
   Purification in the old law did save,
   And such, as yet once more I trust to have
   Full sight of her in Heaven without restraint,
Came vested all in white, pure as her mind.
   Her face was veiled, yet to my fancied sight,
   Love, sweetness, goodness, in her person shined
So clear, as in no face with more delight.
   But O as to embrace me she enclined
   I waked, she fled, and day brought back my night.

When I consider how my light is spent
   Ere half my days in this dark world and wide,
   And that one talent which is death to hide,
   Lodged with me useless, though my soul more
     bent
To serve therewith my Maker, and present
   My true account, lest he returning chide,
   Doth God exact day-labour, light denied?
   I fondly ask; but Patience to prevent
That murmur, soon replies, God doth not need
   Either man's work or his own gifts; who best
   Bear his mild yoke, they serve him best. His
     state
Is kingly. Thousands at his bidding speed
   And post o'er land and ocean without rest:
   They also serve who only stand and wait.

LYCIDAS

In this monody the author bewails a learned friend, unfortunately drowned in his passage from Chester on the Irish seas, 1637. And by occasion foretells the ruin of our corrupted clergy, then in their height.

Yet once more, O ye laurels, and once more
Ye myrtles brown, with ivy never sere,
I come to pluck your berries harsh and crude,
And with forced fingers rude,
Shatter your leaves before the mellowing year.
Bitter constraint, and sad occasion dear,
Compels me to disturb your season due:
For Lycidas is dead, dead ere his prime
Young Lycidas, and hath not left his peer:
Who would not sing for Lycidas? He knew
Himself to sing, and build the lofty rhyme.
He must not float upon his watery bier
Unwept, and welter to the parching wind,
Without the meed of some melodious tear.
  Begin then, sisters of the sacred well
That from beneath the seat of Jove doth spring,
Begin, and somewhat loudly sweep the string.
Hence with denial vain, and coy excuse;
So may some gentle Muse
With lucky words favour my destined urn,
And as he passes turn,
And bid fair peace be to my sable shroud.

For we were nursed upon the self-same hill,
Fed the same flock, by fountain, shade, and rill.

    Together both, ere the high lawns appeared
Under the opening eyelids of the morn,
We drove afield, and both together heard
What time the gray-fly winds her sultry horn,
Battening our flocks with the fresh dews of night,
Oft till the star that rose at evening bright
Toward Heaven's descent had sloped his westering wheel.
Meanwhile the rural ditties were not mute,
Tempered to th'oaten flute;
Rough satyrs danced, and fauns with cloven heel,
From the glad sound would not be absent long,
And old Damoetas loved to hear our song.

    But O the heavy change, now thou art gone,
Now thou art gone, and never must return!
Thee shepherd, thee the woods, and desert caves,
With wild thyme and the gadding vine o'ergrown,
And all their echoes mourn.
The willows, and the hazel copses green,
Shall now no more be seen,
Fanning their joyous leaves to thy soft lays.
As killing as the canker to the rose,
Or taint-worm to the weanling herds that graze,
Or frost to flowers that their gay wardrobe wear,
When first the white thorn blows;
Such, Lycidas, thy loss to shepherds' ear.

    Where were ye nymphs when the remorseless deep
Closed o'er the head of your loved Lycidas?

For neither were ye playing on the steep,
Where your old Bards, the famous Druids lie,
Nor on the shaggy top of Mona high,
Nor yet where Deva spreads her wizard stream:
Ay me, I fondly dream!
Had ye been there – for what could that have done?
What could the Muse herself that Orpheus bore,
The Muse herself, for her inchanting son
Whom universal nature did lament,
When by the rout that made the hideous roar,
His gory visage down the stream was sent,
Down the swift Hebrus to the Lesbian shore.

    Alas! What boots it with uncessant care
To tend the homely slighted shepherd's trade,
And strictly meditate the thankless muse,
Were it not better done as others use,
To sport with Amaryllis in the shade,
Or with the tangles of Neaera's hair?
Fame is the spur that the clear spirit doth raise
(That last infirmity of noble mind)
To scorn delights, and live laborious days;
But the fair guerdon when we hope to find,
And think to burst out into sudden blaze,
Comes the blind Fury with th'abhorred shears,
And slits the thin spun life. But not the praise,
Phoebus replied, and touched my trembling ears:
Fame is no plant that grows on mortal soil,
Nor in the glistering foil
Set off to th'world, nor in broad rumour lies,

But lives and spreads aloft by those pure eyes,
And perfect witness of all-judging Jove;
As he pronounces lastly on each deed,
Of so much fame in Heaven expect thy meed.

O fountain Arethuse, and thou honoured flood,
Smooth-sliding Mincius, crowned with vocal reeds,
That strain I heard was of a higher mood.
But now my oat proceeds,
And listens to the herald of the sea
That came in Neptune's plea;
He asked the waves, and asked the felon winds,
What hard mishap hath doomed this gentle swain?
And questioned every gust of rugged wings
That blows from off each beaked promontory;
They knew not of his story;
And sage Hippotades their answer brings,
That not a blast was from his dungeon strayed,
The air was calm, and on the level brine,
Sleek Panope with all her sisters played.
It was that fatal and perfidious bark
Built in th'eclipse, and rigged with curses dark,
That sunk so low that sacred head of thine.

Next Camus, reverend sire, went footing slow,
His mantle hairy, and his bonnet sedge,
Inwrought with figures dim, and on the edge
Like to that sanguine flower inscribed with woe.
Ah! who hath reft (quoth he) my dearest pledge?
Last came and last did go,
The pilot of the Galilean lake,

Two massy keys he bore of metals twain,
(The golden opes, the iron shuts amain)
He shook his mitred locks, and stern bespake,
How well could I have spared for thee, young swain,
Enow of such as for their bellies' sake,
Creep and intrude, and climb into the fold?
Of other care they little reckoning make,
Than how to scramble at the shearers' feast,
And shove away the worthy bidden guest.
Blind mouths! That scarce themselves know how to
    hold
A sheep-hook, or have learned ought else the least
That to the faithful herdsman's art belongs!
What recks it them? What need they? They are sped;
And when they list, their lean and flashy songs
Grate on their scrannel pipes of wretched straw;
The hungry sheep look up, and are not fed,
But swoln with wind, and the rank mist they draw,
Rot inwardly, and foul contagion spread:
Besides what the grim wolf with privy paw
Daily devours apace, and nothing said.
But that two-handed engine at the door,
Stands ready to smite once, and smite no more.

Return Alpheus, the dread voice is past,
That shrunk thy streams; return Sicilian muse,
And call the vales, and bid them hither cast
Their bells, and flowerets of a thousand hues.
Ye valleys low where the mild whispers use,
Of shades and wanton winds, and gushing brooks,

On whose fresh lap the swart star sparely looks,
Throw hither all your quaint enamelled eyes,
That on the green turf suck the honeyed showers,
And purple all the ground with vernal flowers.
Bring the rathe primrose that forsaken dies.
The tufted crow-toe, and pale jessamine,
The white pink, and the pansy freaked with jet,
The glowing violet.
The musk-rose, and the well attired woodbine.
With cowslips wan that hang the pensive head,
And every flower that sad embroidery wears:
Bid amaranthus all his beauty shed,
And daffadillies fill their cups with tears,
To strew the laureate hearse where Lycid lies.
For so to interpose a little ease,
Let our frail thoughts dally with false surmise.
Ay me! Whilst thee the shores, and sounding seas
Wash far away, where e'er thy bones are hurled,
Whether beyond the stormy Hebrides,
Where thou perhaps under the whelming tide
Visit'st the bottom of the monstrous world;
Or whether thou to our moist vows denied,
Sleepst by the fable of Bellerus old,
Where the great vision of the guarded mount
Looks toward Namancos and Bayona's hold;
Look homeward angel now, and melt with ruth.
And, O ye dolphins, waft the hapless youth.

Weep no more, woeful shepherds, weep no more,
For Lycidas your sorrow is not dead,

Sunk though he be beneath the watery floor,
So sinks the day-star in the ocean bed,
And yet anon repairs his drooping head,
And tricks his beams, and with new spangled ore,
Flames in the forehead of the morning sky:
So Lycidas sunk low, but mounted high,
Through the dear might of him that walked the
    waves,
Where other groves, and other streams along,
With nectar pure his oozy locks he laves,
And hears the unexpressive nuptial song,
In the blest kingdoms meek of joy and love.
There entertain him all the saints above,
In solemn troops and sweet societies
That sing, and singing in their glory move,
And wipe the tears for ever from his eyes.
Now Lycidas the shepherds weep no more;
Henceforth thou art the genius of the shore,
In thy large recompense, and shalt be good
To all that wander in that perilous flood.

    Thus sang the uncouth swain to th'oaks and rills,
While the still morn went out with sandals gray;
He touched the tender stops of various quills,
With eager thought warbling his Doric lay:
And now the sun had stretched out all the hills,
And now was dropt into the western bay;
At last he rose, and twitched his mantle blue:
To-morrow to fresh woods, and pastures new.

Hence loathed Melancholy
  Of Cerberus and blackest midnight born,
In Stygian cave forlorn
  'Mongst horrid shapes, and shrieks, and sights
    unholy,
Find out some uncouth cell,
  Where brooding darkness spreads his jealous
    wings,
And the night-raven sings;
  There under ebon shades, and low-browed
    rocks,
As ragged as thy locks,
  In dark Cimmerian desert ever dwell.
But come thou goddess fair and free,
In Heaven yclept Euphrosyne,
And by men, heart-easing Mirth,
Whom lovely Venus at a birth
With two sister Graces more
To ivy-crowned Bacchus bore;
Or whether (as some sager sing)
The frolic wind that breathes the spring,
Zephir with Aurora playing,
As he met her once a-Maying,
There on beds of violets blue,
And fresh blown roses washed in dew,
Filled her with thee a daughter fair,
So bucksome, blithe and debonair.

Haste thee nymph, and bring with thee
Jest and youthful Jollity,
Quips and Cranks, and wanton Wiles,
Nods, and Becks, and wreathed Smiles,
Such as hang on Hebe's cheek,
And love to live in dimple sleek;
Sport that wrinkled Care derides,
And Laughter, holding both his sides.
Come, and trip it as ye go
On the light fantastic toe,
And in thy right hand lead with thee,
The mountain nymph, sweet Liberty;
And if I give thee honour due,
Mirth, admit me of thy crew
To live with her and live with thee,
In unreproved pleasures free;
To hear the lark begin his flight,
And singing startle the dull night,
From his watch-tower in the skies,
Till the dappled dawn doth rise;
Then to come in spite of sorrow,
And at my window bid good-morrow,
Through the sweet-briar, or the vine,
Or the twisted eglantine.
While the cock with lively din,
Scatters the rear of darkness thin,
And to the stack, or the barn door,
Stoutly struts his dames before;
Oft listening how the hounds and horn

Cheerly rouse the slumbering morn,
From the side of some hoar hill,
Through the high wood echoing shrill.
Sometime walking not unseen
By hedgerow elms, on hillocks green,
Right against the eastern gate,
Where the great sun begins his state,
Robed in flames, and amber light,
The clouds in thousand liveries dight.
While the plowman near at hand,
Whistles o'er the furrowed land,
And the milkmaid singeth blithe,
And the mower whets his scythe,
And every shepherd tells his tale,
Under the hawthorn in the dale.
Straight mine eye hath caught new pleasures
Whilst the landscape round it measures,
Russet lawns, and fallows gray,
Where the nibbling flocks do stray,
Mountains on whose barren breast
The labouring clouds do often rest:
Meadows trim with daisies pied,
Shallow brooks, and rivers wide.
Towers, and battlements it sees
Bosomed high in tufted trees,
Where perhaps some beauty lies,
The cynosure of neighbouring eyes.
Hard by, a cottage chimney smokes,
From betwixt two aged oaks,

Where Corydon and Thyrsis met,
Are at their savoury dinner set
Of herbs, and other country messes,
Which the neat-handed Phillis dresses;
And then in haste her bower she leaves,
With Thestylis to bind the sheaves;
Or if the earlier season lead
To the tanned haycock in the mead,
Sometimes with secure delight
The upland hamlets will invite,
When the merry bells ring round
And the jocund rebecks sound
To many a youth and many a maid,
Dancing in the chequered shade;
And young and old come forth to play
On a sunshine holiday,
Till the livelong daylight fail;
Then to the spicy nut-brown ale,
With stories told of many a feat,
How fairy Mab the junkets ate;
She was pinched and pulled she said,
And he by Friar's lantern led
Tells how the drudging goblin sweat
To earn his cream-bowl, duly set,
When in one night, ere glimpse of morn,
His shadowy flail hath threshed the corn
That ten day-labourers could not end,
Then lies him down, the lubber fiend,
And stretched out all the chimney's length,

Basks at the fire his hairy strength;
And crop-full out of doors he flings
Ere the first cock his matin rings.
Thus done the tales, to bed they creep,
By whispering winds soon lulled asleep.
Towered cities please us then,
And the busy hum of men,
Where throngs of knights and barons bold,
In weeds of peace high triumphs hold,
With store of ladies, whose bright eyes
Rain influence, and judge the prize
Of wit, or arms, while both contend
To win her grace, whom all commend.
There let Hymen oft appear
In saffron robe, with taper clear,
And pomp, and feast, and revelry,
With mask, and antique pageantry,
Such sights as youthful poets dream
On summer eves by haunted stream.
Then to the well-trod stage anon,
If Jonson's learned sock be on,
Or sweetest Shakespeare fancy's child,
Warble his native wood-notes wild,
And ever against eating cares
Lap me in soft Lydian airs,
Married to immortal verse
Such as the meeting soul may pierce
In notes, with many a winding bout
Of linked sweetness long drawn out,

With wanton heed, and giddy cunning,
The melting voice through mazes running;
Untwisting all the chains that tie
The hidden soul of harmony.
That Orpheus' self may heave his head
From golden slumber on a bed
Of heaped Elysian flowers, and hear
Such strains as would have won the ear
Of Pluto, to have quite set free
His half regained Eurydice.
These delights, if thou canst give,
Mirth with thee I mean to live.

Hence vain, deluding joys,
   The brood of folly without father bred.
How little you bestead,
   Or fill the fixed mind with all your toys;
Dwell in some idle brain,
   And fancies fond with gaudy shapes possess,
As thick and numberless
   As the gay motes that people the sunbeams,
Or likest hovering dreams,
   The fickle pensioners of Morpheus' train.
But hail thou goddess, sage and holy,
Hail, divinest Melancholy,
Whose saintly visage is too bright
To hit the sense of human sight;
And therefore to our weaker view,
O'erlaid with black staid Wisdom's hue.
Black, but such as in esteem,
Prince Memnon's sister might beseem,
Or that starred Ethiope queen that strove
To set her beauty's praise above
The sea nymphs, and their powers offended.
Yet thou art higher far descended.
Thee bright-haired Vested long of yore
To solitary Saturn bore;
His daughter she; (in Saturn's reign
Such mixture was not held a stain).
Oft in glimmering bowers and glades

He met her, and in secret shades
Of woody Ida's inmost grove,
While yet there was no fear of Jove.
Come pensive nun, devout and pure,
Sober, steadfast, and demure,
All in a robe of darkest grain,
Flowing with majestic train,
And sable stole of cypress lawn
Over thy decent shoulders drawn.
Come, but keep thy wonted state,
With even step and musing gait,
And looks commercing with the skies,
Thy rapt soul sitting in thine eyes:
There held in holy passion still,
Forget thyself to marble, till
With a sad leaden downward cast,
Thou fix them on the earth as fast.
And join with thee calm Peace, and Quiet,
Spare Fast, that oft with gods doth diet,
And hears the Muses in a ring,
Aye round about Jove's altar sing.
And add to these retired Leisure,
That in trim gardens takes his pleasure;
But first, and chiefest, with thee bring,
Him that yon soars on golden wing,
Guiding the fiery-wheeled throne,
The cherub Contemplation,
And the mute silence hist along
'Less Philomel will deign a song,

In her sweetest, saddest plight,
Smoothing the rugged brow of night,
While Cynthia checks her dragon yoke
Gently o'er th'accustomed oak;
Sweet bird that shunn'st the noise of folly,
Most musical, most melancholy!
Thee chauntress oft the woods among,
I woo to hear thy even-song;
And missing thee, I walk unseen
On the dry smooth-shaven green,
To behold the wandering moon,
Riding near her highest noon,
Like one that had been led astray
Through the Heaven's wide pathless way;
And oft as if her head she bowed,
Stooping through a fleecy cloud.
Oft on a plat of rising ground,
I hear the far-off curfew sound,
Over some wide-watered shore,
Swinging slow with sullen roar;
Or if the air will not permit,
Some still removed place will fit,
Where glowing embers through the room
Teach light to counterfeit a gloom.
Far from all resort of mirth,
Save the cricket on the hearth,
Or the bellman's drowsy charm,
To bless the doors, from nightly harm;
Or let my lamp at midnight hour

Be seen in some high lonely tower,
Where I may oft out-watch the Bear,
With thrice great Hermes, or unsphere
The spirit of Plato to unfold
What worlds, or what vast regions hold
The immortal mind that hath forsook
Her mansion in this fleshly nook;
And of those demons that are found
In fire, air, flood, or under ground,
Whose power hath a true consent
With plane or with element.
Some time let gorgeous tragedy
In sceptred pall come sweeping by,
Presenting Thebes, or Pelops' line,
Or the tale of Troy divine.
Or what (though rare) of later age
Ennobled hath the buskined stage.
But O sad virgin, that thy power
Might raise Musaeus from his bower,
Or bid the soul of Orpheus sing
Such notes as warbled to the string,
Drew iron tears down Pluto's cheek,
And made Hell grant what love did seek.
Or call up him that left half told
The story of Cambuscan bold,
Of Camball, and of Algarsife,
And who had Canacee to wife,
That owned the virtuous ring and glass,
And of the wondrous horse of brass,

On which the Tartar king did ride;
And if ought else great bards beside
In sage and solemn tunes have sung,
Of tourneys and of trophies hung;
Of forests and enchantments drear,
Where more is meant than meets the ear.
Thus night oft see me in thy pale career,
Till civil-suited morn appear,
Not tricked and frounced as she was wont,
With the Attic boy to hunt,
But kerchiefed in a comely cloud,
While rocking winds are piping loud,
Or ushered with a shower still,
When the gust hath blown his fill,
Ending on the rustling leaves,
With minute drops from off the eaves.
And when the sun begins to fling
His flaring beams, me goddess bring
To arched walks of twilight groves,
And shadows brown that Sylvan loves
Of pine, or monumental oak,
Where the rude axe with heaved stroke,
Was never heard the nymphs to daunt,
Or fright them from their hallowed haunt.
There in close covert by some brook,
Where no profaner eye may look,
Hide me from day's garish eye,
While the bee with honeyed thigh,
That at her flowery work doth sing,

And the waters murmuring
With such consort as they keep,
Entice the dewy-feathered sleep;
And let some strange mysterious dream,
Wave at his wings in airy stream,
Of lively portraiture displayed,
Softly on my eyelids laid.
And as I wake, sweet music breathe
Above, about, or underneath,
Sent by some spirit to mortals good,
Or th'unseen genius of the wood.
But let my due feet never fail
To walk the studious cloisters pale,
And love the high embowed roof,
With antique pillars massy proof,
And storied windows richly dight,
Casting a dim religious light.
There let the pealing organ blow,
To the full-voiced quire below,
In service high, and anthems clear,
As may with sweetness, through mine ear,
Dissolve me into ecstasies,
And bring all heaven before mine eyes.
And may at last my weary age
Find out the peaceful hermitage,
The hairy gown and mossy cell,
Where I may sit and rightly spell
Of every star that Heaven doth show,
And every herb that sips the dew

Till old experience do attain
To something like prophetic strain.
These pleasures Melancholy give,
And I with thee will choose to live.

From COMUS

Elder Brother. 'Tis chastity, my brother,
    chastity:
She that has that, is clad in complete steel,
And like a quivered nymph with arrows keen
May trace huge forests, and unharboured heaths,
Infamous hills, and sandy perilous wilds,
Where through the sacred rays of chastity,
No savage fierce, bandit, or mountaineer
Will dare to soil her virgin purity;
Yea there, where very desolation dwells
By grots and caverns shagged with horrid shades,
She may pass on with unblenched majesty,
Be it not done in pride, or in presumption.
Some say no evil thing that walks by night
In fog, or fire, by lake, or moorish fen,
Blue meagre hag, or stubborn unlaid ghost,
That breaks his magic chains at curfew time,
No goblin, or swart faery of the mine,
Hath hurtful power o'er true virginity.
Do ye believe me yet, or shall I call
Antiquity from the old schools of Greece
To testify the arms of chastity?
Hence had the huntress Dian her dread bow
Fair silver-shafted queen for ever chaste,
Wherewith she tamed the brinded lioness
And spotted mountain pard, but set at nought
The frivolous bolt of Cupid; gods and men

Feared her stern frown, and she was queen o' th'
　　woods.
What was that snaky-headed Gorgon shield
That wise Minerva wore, unconquered virgin,
Wherewith she freezed her foes to congealed
　　stone?
But rigid looks of chaste austerity,
And noble grace that dashed brute violence
With sudden adoration, and blank awe.
So dear to Heaven is saintly chastity,
That when a soul is found sincerely so,
A thousand liveried angels lackey her,
Driving far off each thing of sin and guilt,
And in clear dream, and solemn vision
Tell her of things that no gross ear can hear,
Till oft converse with heavenly habitants
Begin to cast a beam on th' outward shape,
The unpolluted temple of the mind,
And turns it by degrees to the soul's essence,
Till all be made immortal: but when lust
By unchaste looks, loose gestures and foul talk,
But most by lewd and lavish act of sin,
Lets in defilement to the inward parts,
The soul grows clotted by contagion,
Imbodies, and imbrutes, till she quite lose
The divine property of her first being.
Such are those thick and gloomy shadows damp
Oft seen in charnel vaults, and sepulchres,
Lingering, and sitting by a new-made grave,

As loath to leave the body that it loved,
And linked itself by carnal sensualty
To a degenerate and degraded state.

* * *

Comus. Nay lady sit; if I but wave this wand,
Your nerves are all chained up in alabaster,
And you a statue; or as Daphne was,
Root-bound, that fled Apollo.
   Lady.   Fool do not boast,
Thou canst not touch the freedom of my mind
With all thy charms, although this corporal rind
Thou hast inmanacled, while Heaven sees good.
  Comus. Why are you vext lady? Why do you
     frown?
Here dwell no frowns, nor anger; from these gates
Sorrow flies far: see here be all the pleasures
That fancy can beget on youthful thoughts,
When the fresh blood grows lively, and returns
Brisk as the April buds in primrose-season.
And first behold this cordial julep here
That flames and dances in his crystal bounds
With spirits of balm, and fragrant syrups mixed.
Not that Nepenthes which the wife of Thone,
In Egypt gave to Jove-born Helena,
Is of such power to stir up joy as this,
To life so friendly, or so cool to thirst.
Why should you be so cruel to yourself,

And to those dainty limbs which nature lent
For gentle usage, and soft delicacy?
But you invert the covenants of her trust,
And harshly deal, like an ill borrower,
With that which you received on other terms,
Scorning the unexempt condition
By which all mortal frailty must subsist,
Refreshment after toil, ease after pain,
That have been tired all day without repast,
And timely rest have wanted. But fair virgin,
This will restore all soon.

  Lady.   'Twill not false traitor,
'Twill not restore the truth and honesty
That thou hast banished from thy tongue with lies.
Was this the cottage, and the safe abode
Thou told'st me of? What grim aspects are these,
These oughly-headed monsters? Mercy guard me!
Hence with thy brewed enchantments, foul deceiver,
Hast thou betrayed my credulous innocence
With visored falsehood, and base forgery,
And wouldst thou seek again to trap me here
With liquorish baits fit to ensnare a brute?
Were it a draft for Juno when she banquets,
I would not taste thy treasonous offer; none
But such as are good men can give good things,
And that which is not good, is not delicious
To a well-governed and wise appetite.

 Comus. O foolishness of men! That lend their ears
To those budge doctors of the stoic fur,

And fetch their precepts from the cynic tub,
Praising the lean and sallow abstinence.
Wherefore did nature pour her bounties forth,
With such a full and unwithdrawing hand,
Covering the earth with odours, fruits, and flocks,
Thronging the seas with spawn innumerable,
But all to please, and sate the curious taste?
And set to work millions of spinning worms,
That in their green shops weave the smooth-haired
    silk
To deck her sons, and that no corner might
Be vacant of her plenty, in her own loins
She hutched th'all worshipped ore, and precious
    gems
To store her children with; if all the world
Should in a pet of temperance feed on pulse,
Drink the clear stream, and nothing wear but
    frieze,
Th'all giver would be unthanked, would be
    unpraised,
Not half his riches known, and yet despised,
And we should serve him as a grudging master,
As a penurious niggard of his wealth,
And live like nature's bastards, not her sons,
Who would be quite surcharged with her own
    weight,
And strangled with her waste fertility;
Th'earth cumbered, and the winged air darkt with
    plumes,

47

The herds would over-multitude their lords,
The sea o'erfraught would swell, and th'unsought
   diamonds
Would so emblaze the forehead of the deep,
And so bestud with stars, that they below
Would grow inured to light, and come at last
To gaze upon the sun with shameless brows.
List lady be not coy, and be not cozened
With that same vaunted name virginity;
Beauty is nature's coin, must not be hoarded,
But must be current, and the good thereof
Consists in mutual and partaken bliss,
Unsavoury in the enjoyment of itself.
If you let slip time, like a neglected rose
It withers on the stalk with languished head.
Beauty is nature's brag, and must be shown
In courts, at feasts, and high solemnities
Where most may wonder at the workmanship;
It is for homely features to keep home,
They had their name thence; coarse complexions
And cheeks of sorry grain will serve to ply
The sampler, and to tease the huswife's wool.
What need a vermeil-tinctured lip for that
Love-darting eyes, or tresses like the morn?
There was another meaning in these gifts;
Think what, and be advised, you are but young
   yet.
   Lady. I had not thought to have unlocked my
   lips

48

In this unhallowed air, but that this juggler
Would think to charm my judgement, as mine eyes,
Obtruding false rules pranked in reason's garb.
I hate when vice can bolt her arguments,
And virtue has no tongue to check her pride:
Impostor do not charge most innocent nature,
As if she would her children should be riotous
With her abundance; she good cateress
Means her provision only to the good
That live according to her sober laws,
And holy dictate of spare temperance:
If every just man that now pines with want
Had but a moderate and beseeming share
Of that which lewdly-pampered luxury
Now heaps upon some few with vast excess,
Nature's full blessings would be well dispensed
In unsuperfluous even proportion,
And she no whit encumbered with her store;
And then the giver would be better thanked,
His praise due paid; for swinish gluttony
Ne'er looks to Heaven amidst his gorgeous feast,
But with besotted base ingratitude
Crams, and blasphemes his feeder. Shall I go on?
Or have I said enough? To him that dares
Arm his profane tongue with contemptuous words
Against the sun-clad power of chastity,
Fain would I something say, yet to what end?
Thou hast nor ear, nor soul to apprehend
The sublime notion, and high mystery

That must be uttered to unfold the sage
And serious doctrine of virginity,
And thou art worthy that thou should'st not know
More happiness than this thy present lot.
Enjoy your dear wit, and gay rhetoric
That hath so well been taught her dazzling fence;
Thou art not fit to hear thyself convinced;
Yet should I try, the uncontrolled worth
Of this pure cause would kindle my rapt spirits
To such a flame of sacred vehemence,
That dumb things would be moved to sympathize,
And the brute earth would lend her nerves, and
    shake,
Till all thy magic structures reared so high,
Were shattered into heaps o'er thy false head.
   Comus. She fables not, I feel that I do fear
Her words set off by some superior power;
And though not mortal, yet a cold shuddering dew
Dips me all o'er, as when the wrath of Jove
Speaks thunder, and the chains of Erebus
To some of Saturn's crew. I must dissemble,
And try her yet more strongly. Come, no more,
This is mere moral babble, and direct
Against the canon laws of our foundation;
I must not suffer this, yet 'tis but the lees
And settlings of a melancholy blood;
But this will cure all straight, one sip of this
Will bathe the drooping spirits in delight
Beyond the bliss of dreams. Be wise, and taste. –

SONG (*from* COMUS)

Sabrina fair
  Listen where thou art sitting
Under the glassy, cool, translucent wave,
  In twisted braids of lilies knitting
The loose train of thy amber-dropping hair;
  Listen for dear honour's sake,
  Goddess of the silver lake,
    Listen and save.

PARADISE LOST
From Book One

Of man's first disobedience, and the fruit
Of that forbidden tree, whose mortal taste
Brought death into the world, and all our woe,
With loss of Eden, till one greater Man
Restore us, and regain the blissful seat,
Sing, Heav'nly Muse, that on the secret top
Of Oreb, or of Sinai, didst inspire
That shepherd who first taught the chosen seed
In the beginning how the heav'ns and earth
Rose out of Chaos; or if Sion hill
Delight thee more, and Siloa's brook that flowed
Fast by the oracle of God, I thence
Invoke thy aid to my advent'rous song,
That with no middle flight intends to soar
Above th' Aonian mount, while it pursues
Things unattempted yet in prose or rhyme.
And chiefly thou, O Spirit, that dost prefer
Before all temples th' upright heart and pure,
Instruct me, for thou know'st; thou from the first
Wast present, and with mighty wings outspread
Dove-like sat'st brooding on the vast abyss
And mad'st it pregnant: what in me is dark
Illumine, what is low raise and support;
That to the highth of this great argument
I may assert Eternal Providence,
And justify the ways of God to men.
  Say first, for heav'n hides nothing from thy view,

Nor the deep tract of hell, say first what cause
Moved our grand parents in that happy state,
Favored of Heav'n so highly, to fall off
From their Creator, and transgress his will
For one restraint, lords of the world besides?
Who first seduced them to that foul revolt?
Th' infernal Serpent; he it was whose guile,
Stirred up with envy and revenge, deceived
The mother of mankind, what time his pride
Had cast him out from heav'n, with all his host
Of rebel angels, by whose aid aspiring
To set himself in glory above his peers,
He trusted to have equaled the Most High,
If he opposed; and with ambitious aim
Against the throne and monarchy of God
Raised impious war in heav'n and battle proud
With vain attempt. Him the Almighty Power
Hurled headlong flaming from th' ethereal sky
With hideous ruin and combustion down
To bottomless perdition, there to dwell
In adamantine chains and penal fire,
Who durst defy th' Omnipotent to arms.
Nine times the space that measures day and
    night
To mortal men, he with his horrid crew
Lay vanquished, rolling in the fiery gulf
Confounded though immortal. But his doom
Reserved him to more wrath; for now the thought
Both of lost happiness and lasting pain
Torments him; round he throws his baleful eyes,

53

That witnessed huge affliction and dismay
Mixed with obdurate pride and steadfast hate.
At once as far as angels ken he views
The dismal situation waste and wild
A dungeon horrible, on all sides round
As one great furnace flamed, yet from those
   flames
No light, but rather darkness visible
Served only to discover sights of woe,
Regions of sorrow, doleful shades, where peace
And rest can never dwell, hope never comes
That comes to all; but torture without end
Still urges, and a fiery deluge, fed
With ever-burning sulphur unconsumed:
Such place Eternal Justice had prepared
For those rebellious, here their prison ordained
In utter darkness, and their portion set
As far removed from God and light of heav'n
As from the center thrice to th' utmost pole.
O how unlike the place from whence they fell!
There the companions of his fall, o'erwhelmed
With floods and whirlwinds of tempestuous fire,
He soon discerns, and welt'ring by his side
One next himself in power, and next in crime,
Long after known in Palestine, and named
Beelzebub. To whom th' Arch-Enemy,
And thence in heav'n called Satan, with bold
   words
Breaking the horrid silence thus began:

'If thou beest he – but O how fall'n! how
    changed
From him, who in the happy realms of light
Clothed with transcendent brightness didst
    outshine
Myriads though bright – if he whom mutual league,
United thoughts and counsels, equal hope
And hazard in the glorious enterprise,
Joined with me once, now misery hath joined
In equal ruin: into what pit thou seest
From what highth fall'n, so much the stronger
    proved
He with his thunder, and till then who knew
The force of those dire arms? Yet not for those,
Nor what the potent Victor in his rage
Can else inflict, do I repent or change,
Though changed in outward luster, that fixed mind
And high disdain, from sense of injured merit,
That with the mightiest, raised me to contend,
And to the fierce contention brought along
Innumerable force of Spirits armed
That durst dislike his reign, and me preferring,
His utmost power with adverse power opposed
In dubious battle on the plains of heav'n,
And shook his throne. What though the field be
    lost?
All is not lost; the unconquerable will,
And study of revenge, immortal hate,
And courage never to submit or yield:

And what is else not to be overcome?
That glory never shall his wrath or might
Extort from me. To bow and sue for grace
With suppliant knee, and deify his power
Who from the terror of this arm so late
Doubted his empire, that were low indeed,
That were an ignominy and shame beneath
This downfall; since by fate the strength of gods
And this empyreal substance cannot fail,
Since through experience of this great event,
In arms not worse, in foresight much advanced,
We may with more successful hope resolve
To wage by force or guile eternal war
Irreconcilable to our grand Foe,
Who now triumphs, and in th' excess of joy
Sole reigning holds the tyranny of heav'n.'

So spake th' apostate Angel, though in pain,
Vaunting aloud, but racked with deep despair;
And him thus answered soon his bold compeer:

'O Prince, O Chief of many thronèd Powers,
That led th' embattled Seraphim to war
Under thy conduct, and in dreadful deeds
Fearless, endangered heav'n's perpetual King,
And put to proof his high supremacy,
Whether upheld by strength, or chance, or fate;
Too well I see and rue the dire event,
That with sad overthrow and foul defeat
Hath lost us heav'n, and all this mighty host
In horrible destruction laid thus low,

As far as gods and heav'nly essences
Can perish: for the mind and spirit remains
Invincible, and vigor soon returns,
Though all our glory extinct, and happy state
Here swallowed up in endless misery.
But what if he our Conqueror (whom I now
Of force believe almighty, since no less
Than such could have o'erpow'red such force as
   ours)
Have left us this our spirit and strength entire
Strongly to suffer and support our pains,
That we may so suffice his vengeful ire,
Or do him mightier service as his thralls
By right of war, whate'er his business be,
Here in the heart of hell to work in fire,
Or do his errands in the gloomy deep?
What can it then avail though yet we feel
Strength undiminished, or eternal being
To undergo eternal punishment?'
   Whereto with speedy words th' Arch-Fiend
     replied:
'Fall'n Cherub, to be weak is miserable,
Doing or suffering: but of this be sure,
To do aught good never will be our task,
But ever to do ill our sole delight,
As being the contrary to his high will
Whom we resist. If then his providence
Out of our evil seek to bring forth good,
Our labor must be to pervert that end,

And out of good still to find means of evil;
Which ofttimes may succeed, so as perhaps
Shall grieve him, if I fail not, and disturb
His inmost counsels from their destined aim.
But see the angry Victor hath recalled
His ministers of vengeance and pursuit
Back to the gates of heav'n; the sulphurous hail
Shot after us in storm, o'erblown hath laid
The fiery surge, that from the precipice
Of heav'n received us falling, and the thunder,
Winged with red lightning and impetuous rage,
Perhaps hath spent his shafts, and ceases now
To bellow through the vast and boundless deep.
Let us not slip th' occasion, whether scorn
Or satiate fury yield it from our Foe.
Seest thou yon dreary plain, forlorn and wild,
The seat of desolation, void of light,
Save what the glimmering of these livid flames
Casts pale and dreadful? Thither let us tend
From off the tossing of these fiery waves,
There rest, if any rest can harbor there,
And reassembling our afflicted powers,
Consult how we may henceforth most offend
Our Enemy, our own loss how repair,
How overcome this dire calamity,
What reinforcement we may gain from hope;
If not, what resolution from despair.'
    Thus Satan talking to his nearest mate
With head uplift above the wave, and eyes

That sparkling blazed; his other parts besides
Prone on the flood, extended long and large
Lay floating many a rood, in bulk as huge
As whom the fables name of monstrous size,
Titanian or Earth-born, that warred on Jove,
Briareos or Typhon, whom the den
By ancient Tarsus held, or that sea-beast
Leviathan, which God of all his works
Created hugest that swim th' ocean stream:
Him haply slumb'ring on the Norway foam,
The pilot of some small night-foundered skiff,
Deeming some island, oft, as seamen tell,
With fixèd anchor in his scaly rind
Moors by his side under the lee, while night
Invests the sea, and wishèd morn delays:
So stretched out huge in length the Arch-Fiend lay
Chained on the burning lake; nor ever thence
Had ris'n or heaved his head, but that the will
And high permission of all-ruling Heaven
Left him at large to his own dark designs,
That with reiterated crimes he might
Heap on himself damnation, while he sought
Evil to others, and enraged might see
How all his malice served but to bring forth
Infinite goodness, grace and mercy shown
On man by him seduced, but on himself
Treble confusion, wrath and vengeance poured.

  Forthwith upright he rears from off the pool
His mighty stature; on each hand the flames

Driv'n backward slope their pointing spires, and
    rolled
In billows, leave i' th' midst a horrid vale.
Then with expanded wings he steers his flight
Aloft, incumbent on the dusky air
That felt unusual weight, till on dry land
He lights, if it were land that ever burned
With solid, as the lake with liquid fire,
And such appeared in hue; as when the force
Of subterranean wind transports a hill
Torn from Pelorus, or the shattered side
Of thund'ring Etna, whose combustible
And fueled entrails thence conceiving fire,
Sublimed with mineral fury, aid the winds,
And leave a singèd bottom all involved
With stench and smoke: such resting found the sole
Of unblest feet. Him followed his next mate,
Both glorying to have scaped the Stygian flood
As gods, and by their own recovered strength,
Not by the sufferance of supernal power.

  'Is this the region, this the soil, the clime,'
Said then the lost Archangel, 'this the seat
That we must change for heav'n, this mournful
    gloom
For that celestial light? Be it so, since he
Who now is sovran can dispose and bid
What shall be right: fardest from him is best,
Whom reason hath equaled, force hath made
    supreme

Above his equals. Farewell, happy fields,
Where joy for ever dwells! Hail, horrors, hail,
Infernal world, and thou, profoundest hell,
Receive thy new possessor: one who brings
A mind not to be changed by place or time.
The mind is its own place, and in itself
Can make a heav'n of hell, a hell of heav'n.
What matter where, if I be still the same,
And what I should be, all but less than he
Whom thunder hath made greater? Here at least
We shall be free; th' Almighty hath not built
Here for his envy, will not drive us hence:
Here we may reign secure, and in my choice
To reign is worth ambition, though in hell:
Better to reign in hell than serve in heav'n.
But wherefore let we then our faithful friends,
Th' associates and copartners of our loss,
Lie thus astonished on th' oblivious pool,
And call them not to share with us their part
In this unhappy mansion, or once more
With rallied arms to try what may be yet
Regained in heav'n, or what more lost in hell?'

PARADISE LOST
From Book Four

O thou that with surpassing glory crowned
Look'st from thy sole dominion like the god
Of this new world; at whose sight all the stars
Hide their diminished heads; to thee I call,
But with no friendly voice, and add thy name,
O sun, to tell thee how I hate thy beams
That bring to my remembrance from what state
I fell, how glorious once above thy sphere;
Till pride and worse ambition threw me down
Warring in heav'n against heav'n's matchless King.
Ah wherefore? He deserved no such return
From me, whom he created what I was
In that bright eminence, and with his good
Upbraided none; nor was his service hard.
What could be less than to afford him praise,
The easiest recompense, and pay him thanks,
How due! Yet all his good proved ill in me,
And wrought but malice; lifted up so high
I sdained subjection, and thought one step higher
Would set me highest, and in a moment quit
The debt immense of endless gratitude,
So burthensome still paying, still to owe;
Forgetful what from him I still received,
And understood not that a grateful mind
By owing owes not, but still pays, at once
Indebted and discharged; what burden then?
O had his powerful destiny ordained

Me some inferior angel, I had stood
Then happy; no unbounded hope had raised
Ambition. Yet why not? Some other Power
As great might have aspired, and me though
  mean
Drawn to his part; but other Powers as great
Fell not, but stand unshaken, from within
Or from without, to all temptations armed.
Hadst thou the same free will and power to stand?
Thou hadst. Whom hast thou then or what to
  accuse,
But Heav'n's free love dealt equally to all?
Be then his love accurst, since love or hate,
To me alike, it deals eternal woe.
Nay cursed be thou, since against his thy will
Chose freely what it now so justly rues.
Me miserable! which way shall I fly
Infinite wrath, and infinite despair?
Which way I fly is hell; myself am hell;
And in the lowest deep a lower deep
Still threat'ning to devour me opens wide,
To which the hell I suffer seems a heav'n.
O then at last relent: is there no place
Left for repentance, none for pardon left?
None left but by submission; and that word
Disdain forbids me, and my dread of shame
Among the Spirits beneath, whom I seduced
With other promises and other vaunts
Than to submit, boasting I could subdue
Th' Omnipotent. Ay me, they little know

How dearly I abide that boast so vain,
Under what torments inwardly I groan;
While they adore me on the throne of hell,
With diadem and scepter high advanced,
The lower still I fall, only supreme
In misery; such joy ambition finds.
But say I could repent and could obtain
By act of grace my former state; how soon
Would highth recall high thoughts, how soon
    unsay
What feigned submission swore: ease would recant
Vows made in pain, as violent and void.
For never can true reconcilement grow
Where wounds of deadly hate have pierced so deep;
Which would but lead me to a worse relapse
And heavier fall: so should I purchase dear
Short intermission bought with double smart.
This knows my Punisher; therefore as far
From granting he, as I from begging peace.
All hope excluded thus, behold instead
Of us outcast, exiled, his new delight,
Mankind created, and for him this world.
So farewell hope, and with hope farewell fear,
Farewell remorse! All good to me is lost;
Evil, be thou my good; by thee at least
Divided empire with heav'n's King I hold
By thee, and more than half perhaps will reign;
As man ere long, and this new world shall know.'

'Awake,
My fairest, my espoused, my latest found,
Heav'n's last best gift, my ever new delight,
Awake, the morning shines, and the fresh field
Calls us; we lose the prime, to mark how spring
Our tended plants, how blows the citron grove,
What drops the myrrh, and what the balmy reed,
How Nature paints her colors, how the bee
Sits on the bloom extracting liquid sweet.'

Such whispering waked her, but with startled eye
On Adam, whom embracing, thus she spake:

'O sole in whom my thoughts find all repose,
My glory, my perfection, glad I see
Thy face, and morn returned, for I this night –
Such night till this I never passed – have dreamed,
If dreamed, not as I oft am wont, of thee,
Works of day past, or morrow's next design,
But of offense and trouble, which my mind
Knew never till this irksome night. Methought
Close at mine ear one called me forth to walk
With gentle voice; I thought it thine. It said:
"Why sleep'st thou, Eve? Now is the pleasant time,
The cool, the silent, save where silence yields
To the night-warbling bird, that now awake
Tunes sweetest his love-labored song; now reigns
Full-orbed the moon, and with more pleasing light

Shadowy sets off the face of things; in vain,
If none regard; heav'n wakes with all his eyes,
Whom to behold but thee, Nature's desire,
In whose sight all things joy, with ravishment
Attracted by thy beauty still to gaze?"
I rose as at thy call, but found thee not;
To find thee I directed then my walk;
And on, methought, alone I passed through ways
That brought me on a sudden to the tree
Of interdicted knowledge. Fair it seemed,
Much fairer to my fancy than by day;
And as I wond'ring looked, beside it stood
One shaped and winged like one of those from
    heav'n
By us oft seen; his dewy locks distilled
Ambrosia; on that tree he also gazed;
And "O fair plant," said he, "with fruit surcharged,
Deigns none to ease thy load and taste thy sweet,
Nor god, nor man; is knowledge so despised?
Or envy, or what reserve forbids to taste?
Forbid who will, none shall from me withhold
Longer thy offered good, why else set here?"
This said he paused not, but with vent'rous arm
He plucked, he tasted; me damp horror chilled
At such bold words vouched with a deed so bold.
But he thus, overjoyed: "O fruit divine,
Sweet of thyself, but much more sweet thus cropped,
Forbidden here, it seems, as only fit
For gods, yet able to make gods of men;

66

And why not gods of men, since good, the more
Communicated, more abundant grows,
The author not impaired, but honored more?
Here, happy creature, fair angelic Eve,
Partake thou also; happy though thou art,
Happier thou may'st be, worthier canst not be;
Taste this, and be henceforth among the gods
Thyself a goddess, not to earth confined,
But sometimes in the air, as we; sometimes
Ascend to heav'n, by merit thine, and see
What life the gods live there, and such live thou."
So saying, he drew nigh, and to me held,
Even to my mouth of that same fruit held part
Which he had plucked; the pleasant savory smell
So quickened appetite that I, methought,
Could not but taste. Forthwith up to the clouds
With him I flew, and underneath beheld
The earth outstretched immense, a prospect wide
And various. Wond'ring at my flight and change
To this high exaltation, suddenly
My guide was gone, and I, methought, sunk down,
And fell asleep; but O how glad I waked
To find this but a dream!' Thus Eve her night
Related, and thus Adam answered sad:
    'Best image of myself and dearer half,
The trouble of thy thoughts this night in sleep
Affects me equally; nor can I like
This uncouth dream, of evil sprung, I fear;
Yet evil whence? In thee can harbor none,

Created pure. But know that in the soul
Are many lesser faculties that serve
Reason as chief; among these fancy next
Her office holds; of all external things,
Which the five watchful senses represent,
She forms imaginations, airy shapes,
Which reason joining or disjoining frames
All what we affirm or what deny, and call
Our knowledge or opinion; then retires
Into her private cell when nature rests.
Oft in her absence mimic fancy wakes
To imitate her; but misjoining shapes,
Wild work produces oft, and most in dreams,
Ill matching words and deeds long past or late.
Some such resemblances methinks I find
Of our last ev'ning's talk in this thy dream,
But with addition strange; yet be not sad.
Evil into the mind of god or man
May come and go, so unapproved, and leave
No spot or blame behind; which gives me hope
That what in sleep thou didst abhor to dream,
Waking thou never wilt consent to do.
Be not disheartened then, nor cloud those looks
That wont to be more cheerful and serene
Than when fair morning first smiles on the world,
And let us to our fresh employments rise
Among the groves, the fountains, and the flow'rs
That open now their choicest bosomed smells
Reserved from night, and kept for thee in store.'

So cheered he his fair spouse, and she was
    cheered,
But silently a gentle tear let fall
From either eye, and wiped them with her hair;
Two other precious drops that ready stood,
Each in their crystal sluice, he ere they fell
Kissed as the gracious signs of sweet remorse
And pious awe, that feared to have offended.
    So all was cleared, and to the field they haste.
But first from under shady arborous roof,
Soon as they forth were come to open sight
Of day-spring, and the sun, who scarce up risen
With wheels yet hov'ring o'er the ocean brim,
Shot parallel to the earth his dewy ray,
Discovering in wide landscape all the east
Of Paradise and Eden's happy plains,
Lowly they bowed adoring, and began
Their orisons, each morning duly paid
In various style, for neither various style
Nor holy rapture wanted they to praise
Their Maker, in fit strains pronounced or sung
Unmeditated; such prompt eloquence
Flowed from their lips, in prose or numerous verse,
More tuneable than needed lute or harp
To add more sweetness, and they thus began:
    'These are thy glorious works, Parent of good,
Almighty, thine this universal frame,
Thus wondrous fair; thyself how wondrous then!
Unspeakable, who sitt'st above these heavens,

To us invisible or dimly seen
In these thy lowest works, yet these declare
Thy goodness beyond thought, and power divine.
Speak ye who best can tell, ye sons of light,
Angels, for ye behold him, and with songs
And choral symphonies, day without night,
Circle his throne rejoicing, ye in heav'n;
On earth join all ye creatures to extol
Him first, him last, him midst, and without end.
Fairest of stars, last in the train of night,
If better thou belong not to the dawn,
Sure pledge of day, that crown'st the smiling morn
With thy bright circlet, priase him in thy sphere
While day arises, that sweet hour of prime.
Thou sun, of this great world both eye and soul,
Acknowledge him thy greater; sound his praise
In thy eternal course, both when thou climb'st,
And when high noon hast gained, and when thou
    fall'st.
Moon, that now meet'st the orient sun, now fli'st
With the fixed stars, fixed in their orb that flies,
And ye five other wand'ring fires that move
In mystic dance not without song, resound
His praise, who out of darkness called up light.
Air, and ye elements, the eldest birth
Of Nature's womb, that in quaternion run
Perpertual circle, multiform, and mix
And nourish all things, let your ceaseless change
Vary to our great Maker still new praise.

Ye mists and exhalations that now rise
From hill or steaming lake, dusky or gray,
Till the sun paint your fleecy skirts with gold,
In honor to the world's great Author rise;
Whether to deck with clouds the uncolored sky,
Or wet the thirsty earth with falling showers,
Rising or falling still advance his praise.
His praise, ye winds, that from four quarters blow,
Breathe soft or loud; and wave your tops, ye pines,
With every plant, in sign of worship wave.
Fountains, and ye that warble, as ye flow,
Melodious murmurs, warbling tune his praise.
Join voices, all ye living souls; ye birds,
That singing up to heaven gate ascend,
Bear on your wings and in your notes his praise;
Ye that in waters glide, and ye that walk
The earth, and stately tread, or lowly creep,
Witness if I be silent, morn or even,
To hill, or valley, fountain, or fresh shade
Made vocal by my song, and taught his praise.
Hail, universal Lord, be bounteous still
To give us only good; and if the night
Have gathered aught of evil or concealed,
Disperse it, as now light dispels the dark.'

PARADISE LOST
From Book Nine

To me shall be the glory sole among
The infernal Powers, in one day to have marred
What he, Almighty styled, six nights and days
Continued making, and who knows how long
Before had been contriving? Though perhaps
Not longer than since I in one night freed
From servitude inglorious well-nigh half
Th'angelic name, and thinner left the throng
Of his adorers. He to be avenged,
And to repair his numbers thus impaired,
Whether such virtue spent of old now failed
More angels to create, if they at least
Are his created, or to spite us more,
Determined to advance into our room
A creature formed of earth, and him endow,
Exalted from so base original,
With heav'nly spoils, our spoils. What he decreed
He effected; man he made, and for him built
Magnificent this world, and earth his seat,
Him Lord pronounced, and, O indignity!
Subjected to his service angel wings,
And flaming ministers to watch and tend
Their earthy charge. Of these the vigilance
I dread, and to elude, thus wrapped in mist
Of midnight vapor glide obscure, and pry
In every bush and brake, where hap may find
The serpent sleeping, in whose mazy folds

To hide me, and the dark intent I bring.
O foul descent! that I who erst contended
With Gods to sit the highest, am now constrained
Into a beast, and mixed with bestial slime,
This essence to incarnate and imbrute,
That to the height of deity aspired;
But what will not ambition and revenge
Descend to? Who aspires must down as low
As high he soared, obnoxious first or last
To basest things. Revenge, at first though sweet,
Bitter ere long back on itself recoils;
Let it; I reck not, so it light well aimed,
Since higher I fall short, on him who next
Provokes my envy, this new favorite
Of Heav'n, this man of clay, son of despite,
Whom us the more to spite his Maker raised
From dust: spite then with spite is best repaid.'
   So saying, through each thicket dank or dry,
Like a black mist low creeping, he held on
His midnight search, where soonest he might find
The serpent. Him fast sleeping soon he found
In labyrinth of many a round self-rolled,
His head the midst, well stored with subtle wiles;
Not yet in horrid shade or dismal den,
Nor nocent yet, but on the grassy herb
Fearless, unfeared, he slept. In at his mouth
The Devil entered, and his brutal sense,
In heart or head, possessing soon inspired
With act intelligential . . .

PARADISE LOST
From Book Nine

So saying, her rash hand in evil hour
Forth reaching to the fruit, she plucked, she eat.
Earth felt the wound, and Nature from her seat
Sighing through all her works gave signs of woe,
That all was lost. Back to the thicket slunk
The guilty Serpent, and well might, for Eve
Intent now wholly on her taste, naught else
Regarded; such delight till then, as seemed,
In fruit she never tasted, whether true
Or fancied so, through expectation high
Of knowledge, nor was Godhead from her thought.
Greedily she engorged without restraint,
And knew not eating death. Satiate at length,
And heightened as with wine, jocund and boon,
Thus to herself she pleasingly began:
   'O sovran, virtuous, precious of all trees
In Paradise, of operation blest
To sapience, hitherto obscured, infamed,
And thy fair fruit let hang, as to no end
Created; but henceforth my early care,
Not without song, each morning, and due praise,
Shall tend thee, and the fertile burden ease
Of thy full branches offered free to all;
Till dieted by thee I grow mature
In knowledge, as the gods who all things know;
Though others envy what they cannot give;
For had the gift been theirs, it had not here

Thus grown. Experience, next to thee I owe,
Best guide; not following thee, I had remained
In ignorance; thou open'st wisdom's way,
And giv'st accéss, though secret she retire.
And I perhaps am secret; Heav'n is high,
High and remote to see from thence distinct
Each thing on earth; and other care perhaps
May have diverted from continual watch
Our great Forbidder, safe with all his spies
About him. But to Adam in what sort
Shall I appear? Shall I to him make known
As yet my change, and give him to partake
Full happiness with me, or rather not,
But keep the odds of knowledge in my power
Without copartner? So to add what wants
In female sex, the more to draw his love,
And render me more equal, and perhaps,
A thing not undesirable, sometime
Superior; for inferior who is free?
This may be well. But what if God have seen,
And death ensue? Then I shall be no more,
And Adam wedded to another Eve
Shall live with her enjoying, I extinct;
A death to think. Confirmed then I resolve,
Adam shall share with me in bliss or woe.
So dear I love him, that with him all deaths
I could endure, without him live no life.'
  So saying, from the tree her step she
      turned,
But first low reverence done, as to the power

That dwelt within, whose presence had infused
Into the plant sciential sap, derived
From nectar, drink of gods. Adam the while
Waiting desirous her return, had wove
Of choicest flow'rs a garland to adorn
Her tresses, and her rural labors crown,
As reapers oft are wont their harvest queen.
Great joy he promised to his thoughts, and new
Solace in her return, so long delayed;
Yet oft his heart, divine of something ill,
Misgave him; he the falt'ring measure felt;
And forth to meet her went, the way she took
That morn when first they parted. By the Tree
Of Knowledge he must pass; there he her met,
Scarce from the tree returning; in her hand
A bough of fairest fruit that downy smiled,
New gathered, and ambrosial smell diffused.
To him she hasted; in her face excuse
Came prologue, and apology to prompt,
Which with bland words at will she thus addressed:

    'Hast thou not wondered, Adam, at my stay?
Thee I have missed, and thought it long, deprived
Thy presence, agony of love till now
Not felt, nor shall be twice, for never more
Mean I to try what rash untried I sought,
The pain of absence from thy sight. But strange
Hath been the cause, and wonderful to hear:
This tree is not as we are told, a tree
Of danger tasted, nor to evil unknown

Op'ning the way, but of divine effect
To open eyes, and make them gods who taste;
And hath been tasted such. The Serpent wise,
Or not restrained as we, or not obeying,
Hath eaten of the fruit, and is become
Not dead, as we are threatened, but thenceforth
Endued with human voice and human sense,
Reasoning to admiration, and with me
Persuasively hath so prevailed, that I
Have also tasted, and have also found
Th' effects to correspond, opener mine eyes,
Dim erst, dilated spirits, ampler heart,
And growing up to Godhead; which for thee
Chiefly I sought, without thee can despise.
For bliss, as thou hast part, to me is bliss;
Tedious, unshared with thee, and odious soon.
Thou therefore also taste, that equal lot
May join us, equal joy, as equal love;
Lest thou not tasting, different degree
Disjoin us, and I then too late renounce
Deity for thee, when fate will not permit.'
   Thus Eve with count'nance blithe her story told;
But in her cheek distemper flushing glowed.
On th' other side, Adam, soon as he heard
The fatal trespass done by Eve, amazed,
Astonied stood and blank, while horror chill
Ran through his veins, and all his joints relaxed;
From his slack hand the garland wreathed for Eve
Down dropped, and all the faded roses shed.

77

Speechless he stood and pale, till thus at length
First to himself he inward silence broke:

'O fairest of creation, last and best
Of all God's works, creature in whom excelled
Whatever can to sight or thought be formed,
Holy, divine, good, amiable, or sweet!
How art thou lost, how on a sudden lost,
Defaced, deflow'red, and now to death devote!
Rather how hast thou yielded to transgress
The strict forbiddance, how to violate
The sacred fruit forbidd'n! Some cursèd fraud
Of enemy hath beguiled thee, yet unknown,
And me with thee hath ruined, for with thee
Certain my resolution is to die;
How can I live without thee, how forgo
Thy sweet converse and love so dearly joined,
To live again in these wild woods forlorn?
Should God create another Eve, and I
Another rib afford, yet loss of thee
Would never from my heart; no, no! I feel
The link of nature draw me: flesh of flesh,
Bone of my bone thou art, and from thy state
Mine never shall be parted, bliss or woe.'

So having said, as one from sad dismay
Recomforted, and after thoughts disturbed
Submitting to what seemed remédiless,
Thus in calm mood his words to Eve he turned:

'Bold deed thou hast presumed, advent'rous Eve,
And peril great provoked, who thus hast dared

Had it been only coveting to eye
That sacred fruit, sacred to abstinence,
Much more to taste it under ban to touch.
But past who can recall, or done undo?
Not God omnipotent, nor fate. Yet so
Perhaps thou shalt not die; perhaps the fact
Is not so heinous now, foretasted fruit,
Profaned first by the Serpent, by him first
Made common and unhallowed ere our taste,
Nor yet on him found deadly; he yet lives,
Lives, as thou saidst, and gains to live as man
Higher degree of life, inducement strong
To us, as likely tasting to attain
Proportional ascent, which cannot be
But to be gods, or angels, demi-gods.
Nor can I think that God, Creator wise,
Though threat'ning, will in earnest so destroy
Us his prime creatures, dignified so high.
Set over all his works, which in our fall,
For us created, needs with us must fail,
Dependent made; so God shall uncreate,
Be frustrate, do, undo, and labor lose,
Not well conceived of God, who though his power
Creation could repeat, yet would be loth
Us to abolish, lest the Adversary
Triumph and say: "Fickle their state whom God
Most favors, who can please him long? Me first
He ruined, now mankind; whom will he next?"
Matter of scorn not to be given the Foe;

However, I with thee have fixed my lot,
Certain to undergo like doom: if death
Consort with thee, death is to me as life;
So forcible within my heart I feel
The bond of nature draw me to my own,
My own in thee, for what thou art is mine;
Our state cannot be severed; we are one,
One flesh; to lose thee were to lose myself.'
    So Adam, and thus Eve to him replied:
'O glorious trial of exceeding love,
Illustrious evidence, example high!
Engaging me to emulate, but short
Of thy perfection, how shall I attain,
Adam? From whose dear side I boast me sprung,
And gladly of our union hear thee speak,
One heart, one soul in both; whereof good proof
This day affords, declaring thee resolved,
Rather than death or aught than death more dread
Shall separate us, linked in love so dear,
To undergo with me one guilt, one crime,
If any be, of tasting this fair fruit,
Whose virtue (for of good still good proceeds,
Direct, or by occasion) hath presented
This happy trial of thy love, which else
So eminently never had been known.
Were it I thought death menaced would ensue
This my attempt, I would sustain alone
The worst, and not persuade thee, rather die
Deserted, than oblige thee with a fact

Pernicious to thy peace, chiefly assured
Remarkably so late of thy so true,
So faithful love unequaled; but I feel
Far otherwise th' event, not death, but life
Augmented, opened eyes, new hopes, new joys,
Taste so divine, that what of sweet before
Hath touched my sense, flat seems to this and
    harsh.
On my experience, Adam, freely taste,
And fear of death deliver to the winds.'
  So saying, she embraced him, and for joy
Tenderly wept, much won that he his love
Had so ennobled, as of choice to incur
Divine displeasure for her sake, or death.
In recompense (for such compliance bad
Such recompense best merits) from the bough
She gave him of that fair enticing fruit
With liberal hand. He scrupled not to eat
Against his better knowledge, not deceived,
But fondly overcome with female charm.
Earth trembled from her entrails, as again
In pangs, and Nature gave a second groan;
Sky loured and, muttering thunder, some sad drops
Wept at completing of the mortal sin
Original; while Adam took no thought,
Eating his fill, nor Eve to iterate
Her former trespass feared, the more to soothe
Him with her loved society, that now
As with new wine intoxicated both

They swim in mirth, and fancy that they feel
Divinity within them breeding wings
Wherewith to scorn the earth. But that false fruit
Far other operation first displayed,
Carnal desire inflaming: he on Eve
Began to cast lascivious eyes, she him
As wantonly repaid; in lust they burn,
Till Adam thus 'gan Eve to dalliance move:

'Eve, now I see thou art exact of taste,
And elegant, of sapience no small part;
Since to each meaning savor we apply,
And palate call judicious; I the praise
Yield thee, so well this day thou hast purveyed.
Much pleasure we have lost, while we abstained
From this delightful fruit, nor known till now
True relish, tasting; if such pleasure be
In things to us forbidden, it might be wished
For this one tree had been forbidden ten.
But come, so well refreshed, now let us play,
As meet is, after such delicious fare;
For never did thy beauty since the day
I saw thee first and wedded thee, adorned
With all perfections, so inflame my sense
With ardor to enjoy thee, fairer now
Than ever, bounty of this virtuous tree.'

So said he, and forbore not glance or toy
Of amorous intent, well understood
Of Eve, whose eye darted contagious fire.
Her hand he seized, and to a shady bank,

Thick overhead with verdant roof embow'red,
He led her nothing loth; flow'rs were the couch,
Pansies, and violets, and asphodel,
And hyacinth, earth's freshest softest lap.
There they their fill of love and love's disport
Took largely, of their mutual guilt the seal,
The solace of their sin, till dewy sleep
Oppressed them, wearied with their amorous play.
Soon as the force of that fallacious fruit,
That with exhilarating vapor bland
About their spirits had played, and inmost powers
Made err, was now exhaled, and grosser sleep
Bred of unkindly fumes, with conscious dreams
Encumbered, now had left them, up they rose
As from unrest, and each the other viewing
Soon found their eyes how opened, and their
     minds
How darkened; innocence, that as a veil
Had shadowed them from knowing ill, was gone . . .

He ended, and they both descend the hill;
Descended, Adam to the bow'r where Eve
Lay sleeping ran before, but found her waked;
And thus with words not sad she him received:
  'Whence thou return'st, and whither went'st, I
     know;
For God is also in sleep, and dreams advise,
Which he hath sent propitious, some great good
Presaging, since with sorrow and heart's distress
Wearied I fell asleep. But now lead on;
In me is no delay; with thee to go,
Is to stay here; without thee here to stay,
Is to go hence unwilling; thou to me
Art all things under heav'n, all places thou,
Who for my wilful crime art banished hence.
This further consolation yet secure
I carry hence; though all by me is lost,
Such favor I unworthy am vouchsafed,
By me the Promised Seed shall all restore.'
  So spake our mother Eve, and Adam heard
Well pleased, but answered not; for now too nigh
Th' Archangel stood, and from the other hill
To their fixed station, all in bright array
The Cherubim descended; on the ground
Gliding metéorous, as ev'ning mist
Ris'n from a river o'er the marish glides,

And gathers ground fast at the laborer's heel
Homeward returning. High in front advanced,
The brandished sword of God before them blazed
Fierce as a comet; which with torrid heat,
And vapor as the Libyan air adust,
Began to parch that temperate clime; whereat
In either hand the hast'ning Angel caught
Our ling'ring parents, and to th' eastern gate
Led them direct, and down the cliff as fast
To the subjected plain; then disappeared.
They, looking back, all th' eastern side beheld
Of Paradise, so late their happy seat,
Waved over by that flaming brand, the gate
With dreadful faces thronged and fiery arms.
Some natural tears they dropped, but wiped them
    soon;
The world was all before them, where to choose
Their place of rest, and Providence their guide:
They hand in hand, with wand'ring steps and slow,
Through Eden took their solitary way.

From SAMSON AGONISTES

Samson. A little onward lend thy guiding hand
To these dark steps, a little further on.
For yonder bank hath choice of sun or shade;
There I am wont to sit, when any chance
Relieves me from my task of servile toil,
Daily in the common prison else enjoined me,
Where I a prisoner chained, scarce freely draw
The air imprisoned also, close and damp,
Unwholesome draught: but here I feel amends,
The breath of Heaven fresh-blowing, pure and
     sweet,
With dayspring born; here leave me to respire.
This day a solemn feast the people hold
To Dagon their sea-idol, and forbid
Laborious works, unwillingly this rest
Their superstition yields me; hence with leave
Retiring from the popular noise, I seek
This unfrequented place to find some ease,
Ease to the body some, none to the mind
From restless thoughts, that like a deadly swarm
Of hornets armed, no sooner found alone,
But rush upon me thronging, and present
Times past, what once I was, and what am now.
O wherefore was my birth from Heaven foretold
Twice by an angel, who at last in sight
Of both my parents all in flames ascended
From off the altar, where an offering burned,

As in a fiery column charioting
His godlike presence, and from some great act
Or benefit revealed to Abraham's race?
Why was my breeding ordered and prescribed
As of a person separate to God,
Designed for great exploits; if I must die
Betrayed, captived, and both my eyes put out,
Made of my enemies the scorn and gaze;
To grind in brazen fetters under task
With this Heaven-gifted strength? O glorious
    strength
Put to the labour of a beast, debased
Lower than bondslave! Promise was that I
Should Israel from Philistian yoke deliver;
Ask for this great deliverer now, and find him
Eyeless in Gaza at the mill with slaves,
Himself in bonds under Philistian yoke;
Yet stay, let me not rashly call in doubt
Divine prediction; what if all foretold
Had been fulfilled but through mine own default,
Whom have I to complain of but my self?
Who this high gift of strength committed to me,
In what part lodged, how easily bereft me,
Under the seal of silence could not keep,
But weakly to a woman must reveal it
O'ercome with importunity and tears.
O impotence of mind, in body strong!
But what is strength without a double share
Of wisdom, vast, unwieldy, burdensome,

Proudly secure, yet liable to fall
By weakest subtleties, not made to rule,
But to subserve where wisdom bears command.
God, when he gave me strength, to shew withal
How slight the gift was, hung it in my hair.
But peace, I must not quarrel with the will
Of highest dispensation, which herein
Hap'ly had ends above my reach to know.
Suffices that to me strength is my bane,
And proves the source of all my miseries;
So many and so huge, that each apart
Would ask a life to wail, but chief of all,
O loss of sight, of thee I most complain!
Blind among enemies, O worse than chains,
Dungeon, or beggary, or decrepit age!
Light the prime work of God to me is extinct,
And all her various objects of delight
Annulled, which might in part my grief have eased,
Inferior to the vilest now become
Of man or worm; the vilest here excel me,
They creep, yet see, I dark in light exposed
To daily fraud, contempt, abuse and wrong,
Within doors, or without, still as a fool,
In power of others, never in my own;
Scarce half I seem to live, dead more than half.
O dark, dark, dark, amid the blaze of noon,
Irrecoverably dark, total eclipse
Without all hope of day!
O first created beam, and thou great Word,

Let there be light, and light was over all;
Why am I thus bereaved thy prime decree?
The sun to me is dark
And silent as the moon,
When she deserts the night
Hid in her vacant interlunar cave.
Since light so necessary is to life,
And almost life itself, if it be true
That light is in the soul,
She all in every part; why was the sight
To such a tender ball as th'eye confined?
So obvious and so easy to be quenched,
And not as feeling through all parts diffused,
That she might look at will through every pore?
Then had I not been thus exiled from light;
As in the land of darkness yet in light,
To live a life half dead, a living death,
And buried; but O yet more miserable!
Myself, my sepulchre, a moving grave,
Buried, yet not exempt
By privilege of death and burial
From worst of other evils, pains and wrongs,
But made hereby obnoxious more
To all the miseries of life,
Life in captivity
Among inhuman foes.
But who are these? for with joint pace I hear
The tread of many feet steering this way;
Perhaps my enemies who come to stare

At my affliction, and perhaps to insult,
Their daily practice to afflict me more.

   Chorus. This, this is he; softly awhile,
Let us not break in upon him;
O change beyond report, thought, or belief!
See how he lies at random, carelessly diffused,
With languished head unpropt,
As one past hope, abandoned
And by himself given over;
In slavish habit, ill-fitted weeds
O'er worn and soiled;
Or do my eyes misrepresent? Can this be he,
That heroic, that renowned,
Irresistible Samson? Whom unarmed
No strength of man, or fiercest wild beast could
    withstand;
Who tore the lion, as the lion tears the kid,
Ran on imbattled armies clad in iron,
And weaponless himself,
Made arms ridiculous, useless the forgery
Of brazen shield and spear, the hammered cuirass,
Chalybean tempered steel, and frock of mail
Adamantean proof;
But safest he who stood aloof,
When insupportably his foot advanced,
In scorn of their proud arms and warlike tools,
Spurned them to death by troops. The bold
    Ascalonite
Fled from his lion ramp, old warriors turned

Their plated backs under his heel;
Or grovelling soiled their crested helmets in the
    dust.
Then with what trivial weapon came to hand,
The jaw of a dead ass, his sword of bone,
A thousand foreskins fell, the flower of Palestine
In Ramath-lechi famous to this day.
Then by main force pulled up, and on his shoulders
    bore
The gates of Azza, post, and massy bar
Up to the hill by Hebron, seat of giants old,
No journey of a sabbath day, and loaded so;
Like whom the gentiles feign to bear up Heaven.
Which shall I first bewail,
Thy bondage or lost sight,
Prison within prison
Inseparably dark?
Thou art become (O worst imprisonment!)
The dungeon of thyself; thy soul
(Which men enjoying sight oft without cause
    complain)
Imprisoned now indeed,
In real darkness of the body dwells,
Shut up from outward light
To incorporate with gloomy night;
For inward light alas
Puts forth no visual beam.
O mirror of our fickle state,
Since man on earth unparalleled!

The rarer thy example stands,
By how much from the top of wondrous glory,
Strongest of mortal men,
To lowest pitch of abject fortune thou art fallen.
For him I reckon not in high estate
Whom long descent of birth
Or the sphere of fortune raises;
But thee whose strength, while virtue was her mate
Might have subdued the earth,
Universally crowned with highest praises.

    Samson. I hear the sound of words, their sense
      the air
Dissolves unjointed, ere it reach my ear.

    Chorus. He speaks, let us draw nigh. Matchless
      in might,
The glory late of Israel, now the grief;
We come thy friends and neighbours not unknown
From Eshtaol and Zora's fruitful vale
To visit or bewail thee, or if better,
Counsel or consolation we may bring,
Salve to thy sores, apt words have power to suage
The tumours of a troubled mind,
And are as balm to festered wounds.

    Samson. Your coming, friends, revives me, for I
      learn
Now of my own experience, not by talk,
How counterfeit a coin they are who friends
Bear in their superscription (of the most
I would be understood). In prosperous days

They swarm, but in adverse withdraw their head
Not to be found, though sought. Ye see, O friends,
How many evils have enclosed me round;
Yet that which was the worst now least afflicts me,
Blindness, for had I sight, confused with shame,
How could I once look up, or heave the head,
Who like a foolish pilot have shipwrackt
My vessel trusted to me from above,
Gloriously rigged; and for a word, a tear,
Fool, have divulged the secret gift of God
To a deceitful woman. Tell me friends,
Am I not sung and proverbed for a fool
In every street, do they not say, how well
Are come upon him his deserts? yet why?
Immeasurable strength they might behold
In me, of wisdom nothing more than mean;
This with the other should, at least, have paired,
These two proportioned ill drove me transverse.

   Chorus. Tax not divine disposal, wisest men
Have erred, and by bad women been deceived;
And shall again, pretend they ne'er so wise.

From SAMSON AGONISTES

Messenger. Occasions drew me early to this city,
And as the gates I entered with sunrise,
The morning trumpets festival proclaimed
Through each high street: little I had dispatched
When all abroad was rumoured that this day
Samson should be brought forth to show the people
Proof of his mighty strength in feats and games;
I sorrowed at his captive state, but minded
Not to be absent at that spectacle.
The building was a spacious theatre
Half round on two main pillars vaulted high,
With seats where all the lords and each degree
Of sort, might sit in order to behold;
The other side was open, where the throng
On banks and scaffolds under sky might stand;
I among these aloof obscurely stood.
The feast and noon grew high, and sacrifice
Had filled their hearts with mirth, high cheer, and
  wine,
When to their sports they turned. Immediately
Was Samson as a public servant brought,
In their state livery clad; before him pipes
And timbrels, on each side went armed guards,
Both horse and foot before him and behind
Archers and slingers, cataphracts and spears.
At sight of him the people with a shout
Rifted the air clamouring their god with praise,

Who had made their dreadful enemy their thrall.
He patient but undaunted where they led him,
Came to the place, and what was set before him
Which without help of eye, might be assayed,
To heave, pull, draw, or break, he still performed
All with incredible, stupendious force,
None daring to appear antagonist.
At length for intermission's sake they led him
Between the pillars; he his guide requested
(For so from such as nearer stood we heard)
As over-tired to let him lean awhile
With both his arms on those two massy pillars
That to the arched roof gave main support.
He unsuspicious led him; which when Samson
Felt in his arms, with head awhile inclined,
And eyes fast fixt he stood, as one who prayed,
Or some great matter in his mind revolved.
At last with head erect thus cried aloud,
Hitherto, lords, what your commands imposed
I have performed, as reason was, obeying,
Not without wonder or delight beheld.
Now of my own accord such other trial
I mean to show you of my strength, yet greater;
As with amaze shall strike all who behold.
This uttered, straining all his nerves he bowed,
As with the force of winds and waters pent,
When mountains tremble, those two massy pillars
With horrible convulsion to and fro,
He tugged, he shook, till down they came and drew

The whole roof after them, with burst of thunder
Upon the heads of all who sat beneath,
Lords, ladies, captains, counsellors, or priests,
Their choice nobility and flower, not only
Of this but each Philistian city round
Met from all parts to solemnize this feast.
Samson with these immixed, inevitably
Pulled down the same destruction on himself;
The vulgar only scaped who stood without.

 Chorus. O dearly-bought revenge, yet glorious!
Living or dying thou hast fulfilled
The work for which thou wast foretold
To Israel, and now li'st victorious
Among thy slain self-killed
Not willingly, but tangled in the fold
Of dire necessity, whose law in death conjoined
Thee with thy slaughtered foes in number more
Than all thy life had slain before.

 Semichorus. While their hearts were jocund and
    sublime,
Drunk with idolatry, drunk with wine,
And fat regorged of bulls and goats,
Chanting their idol, and preferring
Before our living Dread who dwells
In Silo his bright sanctuary.
Among them he a spirit of frenzy sent,
Who hurt their minds,
And urged them on with mad desire
To call in haste for their destroyer;

They only set on sport and play
Unweetingly importuned
Their own destruction to come speedy upon them.
So fond are mortal men
Fallen into wrath divine,
As their own ruin on themselves to invite,
Insensate left, or to sense reprobate,
And with blindness internal struck.

   Semichorus. But he though blind of sight,
Despised and thought extinguished quite,
With inward eye illuminated
His fiery virtue roused
From under ashes into sudden flame,
And as an evening dragon came,
Assailant on the perched roosts,
And nests in order ranged
Of tame villatic fowl; but as an eagle
His cloudless thunder bolted on their heads.
So virtue given for lost,
Depressed, and overthrown, as seemed,
Like that self-begotten bird
In the Arabian woods embossed,
That no second knows nor third,
And lay erewhile a holocaust,
From out her ashy womb now teemed
Revives, reflourishes, then vigorous most
When most unactive deemed,
And though her body die, her fame survives,
A secular bird ages of lives.

Manoa. Come, come, no time for lamentation
  now,
Nor much more cause, Samson hath quit himself
Like Samson, and heroicly hath finished
A life heroic, on his enemies
Fully revenged, hath left them years of mourning,
And lamentation to the sons of Caphtor
Through all Philistian bounds. To Israel
Honour hath left, and freedom, let but them
Find courage to lay hold on this occasion,
To himself and father's house eternal fame;
And which is best and happiest yet, all this
With God not parted from him, as was feared,
But favouring and assisting to the end.
Nothing is here for tears, nothing to wail
Or knock the breast, no weakness, no contempt,
Dispraise, or blame, nothing but well and fair,
And what may quiet us in a death so noble.
Let us go find the body where it lies
Soaked in his enemies' blood, and from the stream
With lavers pure and cleansing herbs wash off
The clotted gore. I with what speed the while
(Gaza is not in plight to say us nay)
Will send for all my kindred, all my friends
To fetch him hence and solemnly attend
With silent obsequy and funeral train
Home to his father's house: there will I build him
A monument, and plant it round with shade
Of laurel ever green, and branching palm,

With all his trophies hung, and acts enrolled
In copious legend, or sweet lyric song.
Thither shall all the valiant youth resort,
And from his memory inflame their breasts
To matchless valour, and adventures high:
The virgins also shall on feastful days
Visit his tomb with flowers, only bewailing
His lot unfortunate in nuptial choice,
From whence captivity and loss of eyes.

Chorus. All is best, though we oft doubt,
What th'unsearchable dispose
Of highest wisdom brings about,
And ever best found in the close.
Oft he seems to hide his face,
But unexpectedly returns
And to his faithful champion hath in place
Bore witness gloriously; whence Gaza mourns
And all that band them to resist
His uncontrollable intent;
His servants he with new acquist
Or true experience from this great event
With peace and consolation hath dismissed,
And calm of mind all passion spent.

PARADISE REGAINED
From Book One

*   *   *   *

Meanwhile the son of God, who yet some days
Lodged in Bethabara where John baptized,
Musing and much revolving in his breast
How best the mighty work he might begin
Of Saviour to mankind, and which way first
Publish his godlike office now mature,
One day forth walked alone, the Spirit leading,
And his deep thoughts, the better to converse
With solitude, till far from track of men,
Thought following thought, and step by step led on,
He entered now the bordering desert wild,
And with dark shades and rocks environed round,
His holy meditations thus pursued:
  'O what a multitude of thoughts at once
Awakened in me swarm, while I consider
What from within I feel myself, and hear
What from without comes often to my ears,
Ill sorting with my present state compared.
When I was yet a child, no childish play
To me was pleasing; all my mind was set
Serious to learn and know, and thence to do
What might be public good; myself I thought
Born to that end, born to promote all truth,
All righteous things. Therefore, above my years,
The Law of God I read, and found it sweet,

100

Made it my whole delight, and in it grew
To such perfection, that ere yet my age
Had measured twice six years, at our great Feast
I went into the Temple, there to hear
The teachers of our Law, and to propose
What might improve my knowledge or their own,
And was admired by all; yet this not all
To which my spirit aspired. Victorious deeds
Flamed in my heart, heroic acts: one while
To rescue Israel from the Roman yoke,
Then to subdue and quell o'er all the earth
Brute violence and proud tyrannic pow'r,
Till truth were freed, and equity restored;
Yet held it more humane, more heavenly, first
By winning words to conquer willing hearts,
And make persuasion do the work of fear;
At least to try, and teach the erring soul
Not wilfully misdoing, but unware
Misled; the stubborn only to subdue.
These growing thoughts my mother soon perceiving,
By words at times cast forth, inly rejoiced,
And said to me apart: "High are thy thoughts,
O Son, but nourish them and let them soar
To what highth sacred virtue and true worth
Can raise them, though above example high;
By matchless deeds express thy matchless Sire.
For know, thou art no son of mortal man;
Though men esteem thee low of parentage,
Thy Father is the Eternal King, who rules

All heaven and earth, angels and sons of men.
A messenger from God foretold thy birth
Conceived in me a virgin; he foretold
Thou shouldst be great and sit on David's throne,
And of thy kingdom there should be no end.
At thy nativity a glorious quire
Of angels in the fields of Bethlehem sung
To shepherds watching at their folds by night,
And told them the Messiah now was born,
Where they might see him; and to thee they came,
Directed to the manger where thou lay'st,
For in the inn was left no better room.
A star, not seen before, in heaven appearing
Guided the wise men thither from the East,
To honor thee with incense, myrrh, and gold,
By whose bright course led on they found the place,
Affirming it thy star new-grav'n in heaven,
By which they knew thee King of Israel born.
Just Simeon and prophetic Anna, warned
By vision, found thee in the Temple, and spake
Before the altar and the vested priest
Like things of thee to all that present stood."
This having heard, straight I again revolved
The Law and Prophets, searching what was writ
Concerning the Messiah, to our scribes
Known partly, and soon found of whom they spake
I am; this chiefly, that my way must lie
Through many a hard assay even to the death,
Ere I the promised kingdom can attain,

Or work redemption for mankind, whose sins'
Full weight must be transferred upon my head.'

        *   *   *   *

  So spake our Morning Star then in his rise,
And looking round on every side beheld
A pathless desert, dusk with horrid shades,
The way he came not having marked, return
Was difficult, by human steps untrod;
And he still on was led, but with such thoughts
Accompanied of things past and to come
Lodged in his breast, as well might recommend
Such solitude before choicest society.
Full forty days he passed — whether on hill
Sometimes, anon in shady vale, each night
Under the covert of some ancient oak
Or cedar to defend him from the dew,
Or harbored in one cave, is not revealed;
Nor tasted human food, nor hunger felt
Till those days ended, hungered then at last
Among wild beasts; they at his sight grew mild,
Nor sleeping him nor waking harmed: his walk
The fiery serpent fled and noxious worm;
The lion and fierce tiger glared aloof.
But now an aged man in rural weeds,
Following, as seemed, the quest of some stray ewe,
Or withered sticks to gather, which might serve
Against a winter's day when winds blow keen
To warm him wet returned from field at eve,
He saw approach, who first with curious eye

Perused him, then with words thus uttered spake:
  'Sir, what ill chance hath brought thee to this
      place
So far from path or road of men, who pass
In troop or caravan, for single none
Durst ever, who returned, and dropped not here
His carcass, pined with hunger and with drouth?
I ask the rather, and the more admire,
For that to me thou seem'st the man whom late
Our new baptizing Prophet at the ford
Of Jordan honored so, and called thee Son
Of God. I saw and heard, for we sometimes
Who dwell this wild, constrained by want, come forth
To town or village nigh (nighest is far),
Where aught we hear, and curious are to hear,
What happens new; fame also finds us out.'
  To whom the Son of God: 'Who brought me hither
Will bring me hence; no other guide I seek.'
  'By miracle he may,' replied the swain,
'What other way I see not; for we here
Live on tough roots and stubs, to thirst inured
More than the camel, and to drink go far,
Men to much misery and hardship born.
But if thou be the Son of God, command
That out of these hard stones be made thee bread;
So shalt thou save thyself and us relieve
With food, whereof we wretched seldom taste.'
  He ended, and the Son of God replied:
'Think'st thou such force in bread? Is it not written

(For I discern thee other than thou seem'st),
Man lives not by bread only, but each word
Proceeding from the mouth of God, who fed
Our fathers here with manna? In the Mount
Moses was forty days, nor eat nor drank,
And forty days Eliah without food
Wandered this barren waste; the same I now.
Why dost thou then suggest to me distrust,
Knowing who I am, as I know who thou art?'
    Whom thus answered th' Arch-Fiend now
      undisguised:
' 'Tis true, I am that Spirit unfortunate,
Who leagued with millions more in rash revolt
Kept not my happy station, but was driv'n
With them from bliss to the bottomless deep;
Yet to that hideous place not so confined
By rigor unconniving, but that oft
Leaving my dolorous prison I enjoy
Large liberty to round this globe of earth,
Or range in th' air, nor from the heav'n of heav'ns
Hath he excluded my resort sometimes.
                *   *   *   *
Men generally think me such a foe
To all mankind: why should I? They to me
Never did wrong or violence, by them
I lost not what I lost; rather by them
I gained what I have gained, and with them dwell
Copartner in these regions of the world,
If not disposer; lend them oft my aid,

Oft my advice by presages and signs,
And answers, oracles, portents and dreams,
Whereby they may direct their future life.
Envy they say excites me, thus to gain
Companions of my misery and woe.
At first it may be; but long since with woe
Nearer acquainted, now I feel by proof
That fellowship in pain divides not smart,
Nor lightens aught each man's peculiar load;
Small consolation then, were man adjoined.
This wounds me most (what can it less?) that man,
Man fall'n, shall be restored, I never more.'

To whom our Saviour sternly thus replied:
'Deservedly thou griev'st, composed of lies
From the beginning, and in lies wilt end,
Who boast'st release from hell, and leave to come
Into the heav'n of heavens. Thou com'st indeed,
As a poor miserable captive thrall
Comes to the place where he before had sat
Among the prime in splendor, now deposed,
Ejected, emptied, gazed, unpitied, shunned,
A spectacle of ruin or of scorn
To all the host of heaven.'

*　*　*　*

So spake our Saviour; but the subtle Fiend,
Though inly stung with anger and disdain,
Dissembled, and this answer smooth returned:

'Sharply thou hast insisted on rebuke,
And urged me hard with doings which not will

106

But misery hath wrested from me; where
Easily canst thou find one miserable,
And not enforced ofttimes to part from truth,
If I may stand him more in stead to lie,
Say and unsay, feign, flatter, or abjure?
But thou art placed above me, thou art Lord;
From thee I can and must submiss endure
Check or reproof, and glad to scape so quit.
Hard are the ways of truth, and rough to walk,
Smooth on the tongue discoursed, pleasing to th' ear,
And tunable as sylvan pipe or song;
What wonder then if I delight to hear
Her dictates from thy mouth? Most men admire
Virtue who follow not her lore. Permit me
To hear thee when I come (since no man comes),
And talk at least, though I despair to attain.
Thy Father, who is holy, wise and pure,
Suffers the hypocrite or atheous priest
To tread his sacred courts, and minister
About his altar, handling holy things,
Praying or vowing, and vouchsafed his voice
To Balaam reprobate, a prophet yet
Inspired; disdain not such access to me.'

    To whom our Saviour, with unaltered brow:
'Thy coming hither, though I know thy scope,
I bid not or forbid; do as thou find'st
Permission from above; thou canst not more.'

    He added not; and Satan, bowing low
His gray dissimulation, disappeared

Into thin air diffused: for now began
Night with her sullen wing to double-shade
The desert, fowls in their clay nests were couched;
And now wild beasts came forth the woods to roam.